3•50

D1465549

The Shropshire & Montgomeryshire Light Railway

Keith & Susan Turner

DAVID & CHARLES
NEWTON ABBOT   LONDON   NORTH POMFRET (VT)

British Library Cataloguing in Publication Data

Turner, Keith
  The Shropshire & Montgomeryshire Light Railway.
  1. Shropshire and Montgomeryshire Light Railway
  – History
  I. Title   II. Turner, Susan
  385'.5'094245   HE3821.S/

  ISBN 0–7153–8233–0

© Keith and Susan Turner 1982

All rights reserved. No part of this
publication may be reproduced, stored in a
retrieval system, or transmitted, in any
form or by any means, electronic,
mechanical, photocopying, recording or
otherwise, without the prior permission of
David & Charles (Publishers) Limited

Photoset by Northern Phototypesetting Co. Bolton
and printed in Great Britain
by Biddles Ltd. Guildford
for David & Charles (Publishers) Limited
Brunel House Newton Abbot Devon

Published in the United States of America
by David & Charles Inc
North Pomfret Vermont 05053 USA

CONTENTS

INTRODUCTION

A journey by rail direct from Shrewsbury to Llanymynech is reminiscent of a past generation. For 30 years the line which links up these two stations had lain derelict, grown over with briar and bramble, and in parts buried in thick brushwood and copse. But in 1911 the old railway, little the worse for its long sleep, once again rattled to the running of the trains, and is now the scene of greater bustle and activity than ever marked its life in the early struggling years of its existence.

(Handbook to Shropshire & Montgomeryshire Railway)

This book is not so much the story of one railway as the chronicle of a number of widely differing schemes – some successful, others not – all following the same or closely similar routes and promoted during the course of more than a century. What started on paper as part of a grandiose rail and sea link between London and Ireland eventually took shape on the ground as a humble branch line soon forced into closure and abandonment. All attempts at resuscitation failed until Colonel Holman Fred Stephens stepped in and rebuilt the line, adding it to a light railway empire unique in this country. At the end of this, the most notable era in the railway's history, the line was taken over and worked by the War Department until the wheel turned full circle for the second time and once again it is no more. But, to return to the beginning . . .

Chapter 1
THE POTTS AND ITS PREDECESSORS

If you lay a ruler across a map of Britain with one end on London and turn it so that it passes through Shrewsbury, the other end will carry on out over North Wales and Anglesey. This fact did not go unnoticed during the days of the Railway Mania and in the 1830s and early 1840s many schemes were considered, and soundly investigated, for laying not a ruler but a direct railway line across the map, linking the capital with a new Irish packet port to be built somewhere in North Wales. Fine on a map but not on the ground, for the mountains of Mid and North Wales proved an insurmountable barrier and in 1844 the Chester & Holyhead Railway was incorporated, killing the dream of a great trunk route through the Welsh Marches.

Less ambitious schemes however prospered and by the early 1860s several lines had either reached Shrewsbury from various directions or were actively in the process of doing so. Running in from the north was the LNWR line from Crewe; from the east the GWR & LNWR joint line from Wellington; from the south-east the GWR from Worcester and Bewdley; from the south the joint line from Hereford and from the west the joint line from the Oswestry & Newtown Railway (later part of the Cambrian) at Buttington, north of Welshpool. All of this clearly meant that Shrewsbury was firmly in the hands of the GWR and LNWR as far as railway traffic went and this situation was to have a considerable influence on the fortunes of the railways described in the following pages.

The West Shropshire Mineral Railway

The first event of direct relevance to the story was the authorisation on 29 July 1862 of the West Shropshire Mineral Railway, promoted by the secretary of the Mid Wales Railway, Richard Samuel France. The plan was for a $13\frac{3}{4}$-mile line from Westbury (11 miles out from Shrewsbury on the Welshpool line) to Llanymynech. Here, close to the Welsh border, France owned the limestone quarries which were to provide the bulk of the railway's traffic. Other possibilities however quickly presented themselves and during the next two years a further four Acts of Parliament were

sought to obtain the necessary powers to construct additional lines; in keeping with this enlarged vision, the company changed its name to the Shrewsbury & North Wales Railway.

The Shrewsbury & North Wales Railway

The proposed line was now rerouted to leave the Welshpool line at Redhill, $2\frac{1}{2}$ miles south of Shrewsbury. At the Llanymynech end a three-mile extension to Llanyblodwel was to serve the Nantmawr lime kilns and from Kinnerley a six-mile branch was to travel south to the Breidden Hills at Criggion to tap the granite quarries there. Other proposals were for further branches from Llanyblodwel to Oswestry and Llangynog up the Tanat Valley. It was now intended to carry passengers as well as minerals, and to this end running powers were sought over the joint line into Shrewsbury General Station; this idea did not receive parliamentary approval though it appears that a premature start was in fact made on the earthworks for the connection at Redhill. Instead, an independent approach into the town was planned by following the Welshpool line closely for much of the way before dropping away down to the London road at Abbey Foregate with a $\frac{1}{2}$ mile spur to connect with the Wellington line. An even more ambitious proposal was made in 1865 for a 14-mile branch from Llanymynech to Llanfair Caereinion but this came to nothing.

With France as contractor work on the undertaking began at the Llanymynech end but before it could be completed events took yet another twist.

The Potteries, Shrewsbury & North Wales Railway

The dreams of certain English companies of reaching the Welsh coast had by no means completely evaporated. One such aspirant was the North Staffordshire Railway which backed the 1865 Shrewsbury & Potteries Junction venture. Its aim was a link between Market Drayton and Shrewsbury. Hoping to expand eastwards, the SNWR expressed interest in some form of joint venture with the SPJR which in turn, hoping to

Shrewsbury Abbey station in the early 1870s with ex-LNWR No 1859 waiting to depart. (*L&GRP*)

expand westwards, reciprocated the hope. The upshot was that on 16 July 1866 the Potteries, Shrewsbury & North Wales Railway appeared, complete with parliamentary approval for the old chestnut of a future extension to Llangynog and thence to Porthmadog. The name of the railway was rather a mouthful and it acquired the nickname of the 'Potts'.

It was a hasty marriage and, like many such, one doomed from the outset. All that came to fruition was the main Shrewsbury–Llanymynech line and the Llanyblodwel and Criggion branches. True, a start was made on the earthworks for the Market Drayton link but in the light of the subsequent fortunes of the company this part of the project was quickly abandoned. Still, the local populace in general – the opposition of the GWR and LNWR notwithstanding – wished it well.

Chapter 2

THE POTTS 1866 – 1880

At last the promoters had something to show for all their efforts – the 'North Wales Section' of the grand design. This intriguing title is in keeping with the fascinating history of this line down the years. The fact that the railway only just managed to creep into Wales – and Mid Wales at that – was blissfully ignored, with fatal results. One wonders exactly how aware the Potts' directors were of the misfit under their control. It served few people in what was, at best, a sparsely-populated area, and went nowhere in the process. Small wonder that it fought a losing battle all its life, succumbing after less than 14 years' service, or, more precisely, 14 years less a temporary suspension of two!

The opening

Announcement of the railway's opening was given in the local press by simple notices such as the one below:

Potteries, Shrewsbury and North Wales Railway.
North Wales Section.
Opening of the line between Shrewsbury and Llanymynech.
The public are respectfully informed that this line of railway, in connection with trains on the Cambrian line to Llanfyllin, Oswestry, etc., will be opened for passenger and goods traffic on Monday, August 13th inst.
For further particulars apply to any of the company's Agents at the stations, or to
J. Bucknall Cooper
General Manager

Offices, Abbey Station,
Shrewsbury,
August 6, 1866.

Left: Abbey station in the 1920s. (*L&GRP*) *Below:* The Abbey station site today.

From the brief account of the opening given in *The Shrewsbury Chronicle* of Friday 17 August no ceremony appears to have taken place; instead the main feature of the day was the running of several excursion trains over the line, conveying large numbers of persons from Shrewsbury to Llanymynech and beyond, and vice versa. The paper noted that 'Numbers of people ascended Llanymynech-hill on Monday; and a good many lovers of the "gentle art" sought sport in the river Vernieu [Vyrnwy], and in most cases met with it, as well filled baskets testified'. The opportunity was taken to wish the railway well with the prediction that it 'will prove acceptable to a rather extensive population, who have hitherto suffered the inconvenience arising from being cut off from railway communication'.

As befitted its aspirations the main line of the railway from Shrewsbury to Llanymynech was laid with double track, though after a more realistic assessment of the situation it was soon singled; the two branches were always single track. Travelling up the line ('up' was officially away from Shrewsbury) the route can be conveniently divided into four separate sections for descriptive purposes: the main line to Kinnerley, the Criggion branch, the main line to Llanymynech and the Nantmawr branch.

Shrewsbury–Llanymynech
The railway's eastern terminus was Shrewsbury Abbey station, opposite the Abbey Church and on the site of the former Abbey Refectory (the pulpit of which stood railed-off in the station yard as a protected monument). In relation to the other lines entering the town the station was to the east of the main GWR route from South Wales to Chester and between the radiating branches to Wellington and the Severn Valley. It was the grandest station on the railway and possessed a two-storey brick building with a verandah and covered platform. The 'platform' on the opposite side of the two terminal roads was at ground level. A trailing junction at the end of one road led to a siding into the Midland Wagon Co's yard while beyond that were sited the two-road locomotive shed, repair shop, turntable and assorted sidings.

The main line left Abbey Station in a direction completely opposite to that needed to reach its generally north-west facing line, and headed south-east, up a severe gradient, for ¼ mile to Coleham Junction where it was joined from the north by a connecting spur from the joint line to Wellington.

This spur provided the only link to another railway at this end of the line and managed to cram into its ½ mile length a high embankment, a two-arch brick bridge over a branch of the River Rea, a girder span over another stream and a deep cutting passing under two roads! The main line now swung through 90 deg to the south-west, crossing the GWR lines to Hartlebury and Hereford on a pair of girder bridges before dropping gently down to parallel the Welshpool line for two miles to Redhill (or Red Hill), three miles from Shrewsbury. Originally the station here boasted two platforms in addition to the usual Potts tiny wooden station building, but when the line was singled one was removed.

Leaving Redhill, the line shortly turned to the north-west, a general direction it adhered to closely all the way to Kinnerley. Immediately crossing the Welshpool line by an embankment and a girder bridge, it entered Hanwood Road station, four miles from Shrewsbury and similar in design and modification to Redhill. The next two stations up the line, Ford (7¼ miles) and Shrawardine (9½ miles), were also similar to the Redhill pattern but retained both platforms and a passing loop when the line was singled. On this whole section were the heaviest earthworks on the railway and culminated in an impressive six-span viaduct of wrought iron girders on cast iron and concrete pillars over the River Severn just before Shrawardine. From here to Kinnerley (13½ miles) the line was virtually level with an intermediate station at Nesscliff (11¾ miles) which, although possessing a brick station building, was not considered worth a loop when the line was singled and so had one platform removed.

The Criggion branch (opened 1871)
Ranking third in importance after Shrewsbury and Llanymynech, Kinnerley was the junction station for the Criggion branch which, while carrying some passenger traffic, was an important source of freight revenue. The branch ran roughly south from the bay platform at Kinnerley, through Melverley (2½ miles) before swinging west across the Severn (and so entering Montgomeryshire) by a seemingly rickety wooden viaduct. (Compared with Brunel's designs for such structures Melverley viaduct was of a decidedly ugly and unsound appearance.) The stations of Crew Green (3½ miles) and Llandrinio Road (five miles) came next as the line turned slowly south-west to reach Criggion, six miles from the junction. The whole

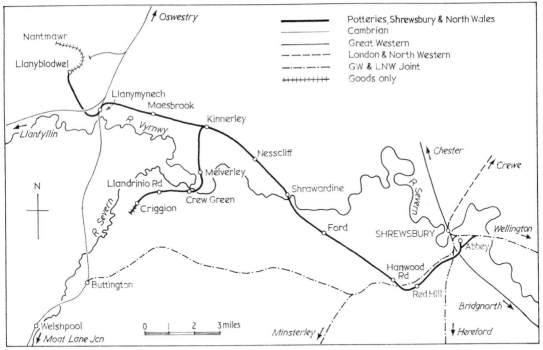

branch was comparatively level and was equipped with simple wooden station buildings, except, for some strange reason, Melverley which boasted a brick structure.

Kinnerley–Llanymynech

Between Kinnerley and Llanymynech the main line ran north-west in virtually a straight line with one intermediate station, Maesbrook, 16 miles from Shrewsbury. Here again was the usual wooden station and two platforms reduced to one. Llanymynech itself was two miles further on and the Potts line curved in from the north to its own platform alongside the Cambrian's double tracks. The Potts' facilities consisted of a wooden building, with a verandah, on the platform, an engine shed and a turntable.

The Nantmawr branch (opened 1872)

The Nantmawr branch supplied the limestone traffic which, despite all pretences in other directions, was the principal reason for the construction of the railway. The branch was reached by using Cambrian metals (over which the PSNW had running powers for this section) which were joined just south of the station by a double junction. Nantmawr trains then almost immediately turned northwards onto the branch proper, gradually swinging north-west under the Cambrian's Llanfyllin branch, over the River Tanat by a wooden viaduct, under a main road bridge, across the river again on a second wooden viaduct and into Llanblodwel, three miles from Llanymynech. The station building was another simple wooden structure; from here an extension curved north-west for about a mile to France's quarries.

Just over a mile of this branch at the Llanymynech end, including a bridge under the Shropshire Union Canal, was in Montgomeryshire. The remainder of the branch, like the rest of the Potts (with the exception of the above-mentioned portion of the Criggion branch), was firmly planted in Shropshire in tacit negation of the extreme claims of the railway's official title.

A slight setback

Before the year was out the Potts was in serious trouble, trouble which arose from legal action taken by an angry debenture holder who, having unsuccessfully demanded his dues, obtained a writ against the company which resulted in the sheriff's officers entering and formally taking possession of Abbey station and the rest of the line on Monday 3 December 1866. No sooner had this taken place than a down train arrived, to be promptly seized by the bailiffs without warning to either the railway staff or the waiting passengers. Only after some bitter haggling was the train allowed to leave, accompanied by one of the bailiffs, though similar requests in regard to other trains scheduled for the day (fair day at Shrewsbury) were refused and normal services were not resumed until the evening.

All trains from then on ran in the official possession of a bailiff comfortably settled in a first class carriage. It seems that this gentleman was afforded every politeness by the railway's employees, though the amusing events of the first night give a better indication of their feelings towards him. Upon arrival at Llanymynech he was moved by a very courteous guard to another compartment which, he was politely informed, had been set aside for his sole use. The bailiff ensconced himself and the train set off back towards Shrewsbury. At Kinnerley some protracted shunting, followed by a lengthy period of apparent inactivity, finally aroused the bailiff's suspicions. Putting his head out of the window he was just in time to see the rest of the train disappearing into the distance. Clambering down, he made for the station, which he found locked, in strict accordance with the regulations, after the passage of the last down train. The unfortunate officer did not reach Shrewsbury, somewhat footsore, until after midnight; there he was apologetically informed that during the shunting operations at Kinnerley the coupling chain between the rear coach − the bailiff's − and the penultimate one somehow, completely by accident, had become unhooked, and somehow, again completely by accident, the fact that the rear coach had been left behind had escaped detection. The bailiff had no choice but to accept this story, though on all subsequent journeys he carefully avoided the rear carriage!

In the event the bailiff's later journeys were comparatively few in number for a hurried meeting of the shareholders was held that same month; it transpired that a working loss of £99 had been made during 1866 and it was resolved to suspend all services temporarily and to realise some of the company's assets. To this end William Hall, a Shrewsbury auctioneer, was instructed to dispose of five locomotives, some rolling stock and various effects from the stations. The sales were conducted by private negotiations and it appears that in fact buyers were found for only three of the engines. As from 21 December the railway lay dormant, a prophetic omen for its future.

A downhill struggle

No further services ran for two years during which time financial matters were put in hand, amalgamation with a number of other small Welsh railway companies was considered and rejected, application was made to Parliament for a time extension for the construction of the Llanyblodwel branch and a similar application was made for rerouting the proposed spur from Abbey station over the Wellington line to connect with the envisaged Market Drayton link. A token start was in fact made on this spur but that was all.

Public services were resumed in December 1868 but on a reduced level. It was a 'main line only' service, for the Criggion branch did not open until 2 June 1871 and the Llanyblodwel branch not until the following year. During the suspension of services it is believed that the decision was taken to carry out the singling of the line already mentioned. It is not known for certain when this was actually done; at the Annual General Meeting in March 1873 it was stated that some of the rails had been sold and the money invested in 'the purchase of 80 wagons, which were urgently required for the purposes of the traffic'. At first it seemed that such economies were paying off and, with the opening of the two branches at long last, it was thought that the stone traffic would be the salvation of the railway. Alas, despite the annual statements of wild optimism, profits during the early 1870s were never more than a few hundred pounds at the very most − and that was on an investment now nearing the £1½ million mark. From then on it was downhill all the way and by the mid 1870s the railway was losing money heavily, in spite of further economy measures such as a reduction in staff and the incentive of reduced fares, though increased journey times did nothing to help. (By 1880 the journey from Llanyblodwel to Shrewsbury could take up to almost two hours.) Passenger figures did actually improve for a while but not sufficiently to prevent the appointment of an Official Receiver in 1877.

The rate of the railway's decline now accelerated. Staffing levels were cut to below the point at which the basic level of maintenance could be performed; in 1880 the Board of Trade imposed a 25mph speed limit until the standard of the permanent way was improved. It never was. Services were cut again. For a while it seemed that the LNWR might acquire the line as it had never really given up its private dream of reaching the

Mid Wales coast, but it was not to be. From 22 June 1880 all services were suspended by the Board of Trade, the track not having been repaired, in the interests of public safety.

It should be mentioned here that considerable confusion exists over exactly when the Nantmawr and Criggion branches opened, some sources implying that both did so on the same date as the main line, 13 August 1866, but for goods services only. If this was the case, it is hard to account for the fact that several years were allowed to elapse, as shown by the official record, before being 'reopened'. It has also been stated elsewhere that passenger services were extended to Llanyblodwel in April 1870; again, this is not borne out by official sources. On the other hand, it is difficult to see why Nantmawr quarries, the railway's most important single source of freight revenue, took so long to be connected with it; the mystery deepens with the mention in the railway's accident returns of the death of a goods guard, run over and killed at Nantmawr whilst shunting, on 19 December 1867 when the line was officially closed! Possibly the explanation is that France was actually working the branch himself to provide his quarries with an outlet, and that the arrangement was not strictly above board.

Services & fares

As seemingly with everything else to do with the railway, the Potts' passenger train service went steadily downhill throughout its life. To begin with there were five trains each way on weekdays and two on Sundays. The first was the obligatory 'Parliamentary' and left Shrewsbury at 6.00am and Llanymynech at 7.05. Journey time was 55 minutes with a stop at every station; the others on the timetable (except on Sundays) ran 10–15 minutes quicker by omitting certain stops in haphazard fashion. During the winter of 1866 one of the weekday trains was dropped before services were suspended.

With the reopening of the line in 1868 the timetable was pruned further with three trains on weekdays and only one on Sundays; Saturday however boasted four! All trains now ran to Llanyblodwel while connections were made at Kinnerley for the Criggion branch. During the period of receivership economies resulted in the issuing of tickets by the guard while the alarming condition of Melverley viaduct resulted in trains running on the branch on Wednesdays, Saturdays and Sundays only.

Travellers on the Potts had a choice of four different rates of fares during most of the railway's life; first, second and third classes were charged respectively 2⅔d, 2d and 1½d per mile, but journeys on the Parliamentary trains were charged at the basic rate of just 1d per mile. In addition, cheap tickets to Shrewsbury were issued on market days and three-day weekend returns to Aberystwyth were also to be had.

From 2 February 1875 second class was abolished on the railway and first and third class rates were reduced to 2d and 1d per mile; first class returns were priced at the old single rate of 2⅔d. Further attempts to attract custom included special cheap day excursion tickets to Llanymynech and Criggion.

Contractor's locomotives

The history of the locomotives of the Potts is difficult to untangle and there remain several tantalising gaps in the story. When the line opened the company had insufficient capital left with which to purchase new locomotives and so drew up an agreement with the contractor, France, under which he supplied 10 secondhand engines of his own. Several (though probably not all) were already on the line, having been used on construction.

In December 1866, as mentioned above, five of these locomotives were put up for sale, but stock returns for the period 1867 to 1872 give a constant stud of seven, indicating that probably only three were disposed of. Details of individual engines follow in order of construction date.

Nantmawr

Nantmawr was built in 1864 by Henry Hughes & Co of Loughborough, a firm later better known for its tramway locomotives. It was a small 0–4–0 saddle tank with 3ft wheels and 10in x 15in outside cylinders. Wooden brake blocks acted on the rear wheels. It had no cab, no dome and no buffers, though it was fitted with heavy beams for shunting contractor's wagons. It was too small and underpowered for regular work on the Potts and was used solely on ballast working. The only change carried out by the railway appears to have been the repositioning of the regulator lever across the firebox from its original vertical position. In 1873 it was sold to Walker Bros of Wigan, then later to Messrs Wood & Wright of Stockton; in 1877 it moved again, in part payment for another engine, to I. W. Boulton's works at Ashton-under-Lyne where it became one of the residents on the famous 'Boulton's Siding'. Repaired by Boulton, *Nantmawr* was hired out on several contracts, eventually going on a permanent basis to the Girvan & Portpatrick Railway in Scotland where it became that line's No 4.

Breidden

This 0–4–0 well tank was built c1865 by Hawthorns of Leith, presumably going straight to France. It had 3ft 8in solid wheels and 12in x 18in cylinders with outside Stephenson's link motion. The water tank was situated between the frames and was filled near the smokebox. Like *Nantmawr* it was used on ballast trains though occasionally it was pressed into service for light passenger and goods workings. It too was sold in 1873 to Walker Bros (and rebuilt as an 0–4–0 saddle tank No 440) then to Messrs Hall Bros & Shaw of the West Bank Alkali Works, Widnes. It was reported in 1920 as still being at work in a colliery near Wigan.

Alyn

This was one of at least four Manning Wardle locomotives supplied to France in 1865. Works No 140, it was an 0–6–0 saddle tank with 3ft wheels and 12in x 17in inside cylinders. Wheelbase was 10ft 9in. Whether or not it was included in the Potts' original 10 locomotives is doubtful for after the construction of the line France sold it (by August 1867) for £800 to another contractor, James Taylor, for use on the latter's contract for the Mawddwy Railway in Mid Wales. Here it took the name *Mawddwy*, later becoming Cambrian Railways No 30 and later still GWR No 824 upon its transfer to the Van Railway. It was scrapped in October 1940 just before closure of this line. During its middle years it was rebuilt twice: once in 1893 and again in 1911.

Powis

This was Manning Wardle 151 of 1865, an 0–6–0 tank with 3ft 10in wheels and 15in x 22in inside cylinders. It survived on the Potts until the sale of stock in 1888 (see Chapter 3).

Sir Watkin

Manning Wardle 167 of 1865, this was another 0–6–0 tank of similar wheel and cylinder dimensions to *Powis*. Presumably they were both of the same class, for later reports show that several parts of 167's motion were found to be

stamped 151, indicating that some rebuilding, using parts from its sister engine, had taken place. It was sold sometime between 1872 and 1874 to the Norton Cannock Colliery Co Ltd, in Staffordshire, moving c1910 to the Astley & Tyldesley Colliery Co where, at Bedford Colliery, it took the name *Bedford*. Later still it worked at several collieries owned by Manchester Collieries Ltd, ending its life on the scrap heap at Walkden Yard in August 1950, by which time a cab had been added.

Viscount/Bradford

Viscount was an identical engine to the above two and was works No 168 of 1865. It lasted until closure of the Potts (by now carrying the name *Bradford*) and was sold in 1888. It was later reported as being at the Blaenavon Iron & Steel Co of Pontypool.

Tanat

Little is known about this locomotive beyond the fact that it was an 0–4–2 tank engine with 3ft 6in driving wheels and 10in diameter cylinders. It too survived on the Potts until 1888.

Of the other four locomotives from the original stock of 10 ex-France engines nothing is known. (If *Alyn* is included in those 10 then of course only three remain to be chronicled.)

Potts locomotives

Apart from the engines obtained from France, two others were purchased by the railway, both arriving in 1872. They were:

1859

This locomotive began life in 1848 as a Bury, Curtis & Kennedy 0–4–2 tender engine constructed for the Southern Division of the LNWR as one of a batch of six. It was equipped with 5ft driving wheels, 3ft trailing wheels, 16in x 24in cylinders and a domeless boiler. It was sold by the LNWR to the Potts in May 1872, by which time its original number 654 had changed firstly to 1154 and then again to 1859. Its stay on the line was however brief and by 1875 it had disappeared to an unknown destination.

Hope

Hope was works No 185 of the Yorkshire Engine Co of Sheffield. In design it was a 2–4–0 tank with 5ft driving wheels, 3ft leading wheels and

16in x 22in cylinders. It was kept until the sale of stock in 1888 when it passed to the East & West Junction Railway and from there to B. P. Blockley, a dealer of Bloxwich, Staffs. In 1905 it was sold to the Cannock & Rugeley Colliery Co which numbered it 8 and renamed it *Harrison*. It was rebuilt in 1916 as an 0–6–0 tank and remained in National Coal Board Service at Rawnsley until scrapped in 1955.

There now comes the problem of trying to assemble the above known details of all the PSNWR locomotives into a plausible whole with reference to the company's official returns. What follows seems to be the most likely account of all the comings and goings.

France carried out the construction of the line with an unknown number of locomotives, including *Alyn*. Upon completion of the contract he sold *Alyn* to Taylor, leaving behind *Nantmawr, Breidden, Powis, Sir Watkin, Viscount, Tanat* and four unknown engines – a total of 10 (not all of which may have been on the line from the commencement of the work, or indeed during any of it). In December 1866 the Potts put five up for sale but only succeeded in disposing of three of the unknown engines. This left the seven shown in the returns until 1873 when the figure of six is given. This can be accounted for by the 1872 sales of *Nantmawr* and *Breidden* and the purchase of No 1859 and *Hope*, followed by the sale in 1873 of *Sir Watkin*. Returns for 1874 give a total of five locomotives, accounted for by the sale of No 1859. By 1875 the number was down to four, accounted for by the sale of the remaining unknown locomotive; this left the final survivors *Bradford, Hope, Powis* and *Tanat*.

Livery used by the PSNWR for its locomotives was originally green and later black, though no doubt there were exceptions to this broad rule; definite details unfortunately do not survive.

Rolling stock

Passenger

Travellers on the Potts were provided with what must have been very uncomfortable four-wheeled four-compartment carriages, possibly ex-LNWR, with small windows and spartan interiors. Company returns give an original total of 21 coaches, reduced to 16 (including three guard's vans) after the 1866 sales and again to just six (including one guard's van) in 1877. The original stock of 21 vehicles was made up thus:

1st class carriages:	4
2nd class carriages:	5
3rd class carriages:	6
Composite carriages:	3
Guard's vans:	3

Judging by available photographs, the different types of passenger coach differed slightly in design while the guard's vans had a birdcage roof and side duckets. They started life on the Potts in a livery of green lower panels and white or cream upper bodywork but weathered in tune with the locomotives to a dull grey colour, probably because there was little money to allow repainting.

Goods

Indicative of the comparative importance of freight receipts, the returns for goods vehicles show a markedly different pattern from those of the passenger stock. The railway began operation with 211 goods wagons and finished with 264, while from 1872 to 1875 no less than 373 vehicles were mentioned. (It should be noted that these were the official figures which often differed from the actual state of affairs: only 188 were actually included in the 1888 auction, plus one known survivor of the sale.)

The fleet consisted primarily of 6ton open trucks for quarry traffic (126 at the auction) together with a smaller number of 8ton trucks (24) for the same purpose. In addition, other traffic was catered for by a range of different vehicles (figures in parentheses are again those included in the auction): 8ton lime trucks (14); 6ton timber wagons (10); cattle trucks (2) and brake vans (2). The survivor of the auction was a 6ton truck at Kinnerley later pressed into service by the enterprising Colonel Stephens.

In addition to this range of vehicles was a 5ton travelling hand crane which comprised the railway's breakdown, maintenance and general odd-job unit, and a hand-worked inspection trolley used by the permanent way gang. Judging by the official returns, it would seem that the crane was purchased in 1868 or 1869.

Chapter 3

IN LIMBO 1880 – 1907

With the PSNWR in the hands of the Receiver the story of the railway now enters a phase as bizarre as any which had preceded or was to follow it; for over a quarter of a century the major portion of the line remained closed and generally decaying, despite all efforts to get it working again before it was, incredibly, resuscitated. This event was however many years distant from the scene of 1880 after the 'suspension' of services for the second time. Some attempt at least appears to have been made to assemble the stock for storage, for all four locomotives were placed in the shed at Shrewsbury, the carriages were lined up in a siding there and the majority of goods vehicles were gathered there and at Coleham Junction sidings on the Wellington line spur. The remainder of the wagons were abandoned at various stations along the line and there they remained, increasingly isolated by rusting points and sprouting undergrowth.

Of the Potts former staff, only a handful of men were kept on by the Receiver to maintain the railway and its stock but it was an impossible task. Buildings quickly fell derelict – the wooden ones rotted away – and rampant vegetation engulfed the track. The timber flooring of the bridges went the way of the other wooden structures and the passenger coaches became the targets for vandalism; only the goods wagons seemed to have weathered well. Basically, beneath the greenery, the permanent way and engineering works suffered little. As for the locomotives, they came off best of all as the first maintenance priority.

The railway was enjoying a ghost existence; it had the stock, it had the track – but it had no services. This sense of isolation from reality can only have been enhanced by the lifting of the Abbey Foregate spur and the erection of a fence across the trackbed. Although one link with the outside world had gone the railway was widely regarded locally as merely suffering an unfortunate setback; it was but a temporary obstacle to overcome for which plans were already being laid.

The Shropshire Railways Co

The first attempt to salvage something from the mess came on the day of closure itself when France offered to the Cambrian the line's major asset, the Nantmawr quarry traffic. Of course France was not a disinterested party since he owned the quarries and had to have an outlet for its product. The Cambrian duly considered this proposal, decided that it might be a profitable move and concluded an agreement dated 28 January 1881 with the PSNWR Receiver whereby the CR would work and maintain the branch for two years. This arrangement started on 1 June that year with the CR paying the PSNWR a royalty of 3d per ton carried. The experiment was obviously to the CR's liking and the agreement was later renewed (though successful bargaining led to a reduction of the toll to 2d per ton as from 1 January 1886).

At the same time it was clear that local feeling was unwilling to let the line simply fade away. There was considerable support for the idea of a direct link with the Potteries and a Bill was prepared to authorise the take-over of the PSNWR and the construction of such a line. On 14 March 1888 the long-suffering shareholders of the old company agreed to accept £350,000 in shares in the new concern, to be known as the Shropshire Railways Co, in the discharge of their dues. The company's engineer, John Russell, put the costs of the venture at £100,000 of which £27,000 would be spent on the Shrewsbury–Llanymynech line, £3,000 on the Llanyblodwel line and £11,000 on the Criggion branch. The Potteries connection would be made by way of a new line from Shrewsbury to Hodnet on the GWR Wellington–Market Drayton line and then via North Staffordshire metals to Stoke. When the Shropshire Railways Act was finally passed on 7 August 1888 the GWR had succeeded in denying the Shropshire Railways running powers to Market Drayton and despite an Act three years later for more time, the extension never amounted to more than just another line on the map.

The capital to be raised for the whole scheme was to be £350,000 in shares (for the Potts shareholders) and £150,000 in debentures to provide immediate finance. Virtually the last act of the Potts was to dispose of its moveable assets, which the SR did not wish to inherit, and provide a clean base on which the new owners could build. Accordingly Mr Alex Young, the Potts liquidator,

Ford (renamed Crossgates) station, 1903, looking west. (*L&GRP*)

arranged a public auction of the railway's stock for Friday 24 August 1888.

The auction

The auction was carried out by the Sunderland firm of Arthur T. Crow and began on the Friday morning by the upper railway bridge at Abbey Foregate where most of the stock was stored. Two of the conditions of sale were slightly unusual and were commented upon in the local press; the first was that the purchasers had to pay the auctioneers

Shrawardine viaduct in SR days. (*L&GRP*)

5% of the lot money on the successful bid — presumably a device to save the company paying commission to the auctioneers — while the second was that purchasers had to remove their lots at their own expense within six days.

A large crowd gathered both to buy and to watch. The proceedings opened with the sale of a score of 6ton trucks; bidding started at £1 each and finished at £3 10s (£3.50). There then followed 35 similar wagons which fetched £3 12s 6d (£3.62$\frac{1}{2}$) each. Bidding was now hotting up and a body went for £1 15s (£1.75), followed by 21 8ton trucks for the grand sum of £7 each. Then came a lime wagon body for £1 and a pair of timber wagons for £4 15s (£4.75) each before the gathering moved up the line a short way to Coleham Junction where 10 6ton trucks went for

£4 each, nine of the same made £3 17s 6d (£3.87½) each, two lime wagons fetched £7 each and a pair of timber wagons each made £4 10s (£4.50).

The auction now moved down to Abbey station yard where more goods vehicles were sold. Five 6ton trucks made £3 15s (£3.75) each and three 8ton trucks £5 each. A cattle truck went for £6 5s (£6.25), as did a brake van. The railway's travelling crane, without its truck, fetched £54. Moving on to the adjacent Midland Wagon Co's yard, 14 6ton trucks made £4 each, seven lime wagons £5 12s 6d (£5.62½) each, six timber wagons £4 15s (£4.75) each, a cattle wagon £5 15s (£5.75) and a goods van £8. Then came a 6in single cylinder pumping engine which made only £7 before the major attractions – the locomotives – were reached. The bidding for *Powis* started at £50 and finished at £210; *Hope* went from £75 to £200; *Tanat* from £50 to £85 and lastly, a lot including *Bradford* (described as 'not complete') started at £100 and reached no less than £305. These prices presumably reflected the comparative conditions of the engines; in view of its price and description it is tempting to suppose that *Bradford* was in the middle of an overhaul and therefore in a better state of repair than its companions.

With all stock now disposed of at the Shrewsbury end of the line, the auction was transferred station by station up the railway. Details of these sales are tabulated below.

Ford: 9 6ton trucks @ £3 10s (£3.50)
Shrawardine: 2 6ton trucks @ £4
                   1 lime wagon @ £4
Nesscliff: 4 6ton trucks @ £3 10s (£3.50)
Kinnerley: 6 6ton trucks @ £3 2s 6d(£3.12½)
Llanymynech: 10 6ton trucks @ £4 10s (£4.50)
                  2 lime wagons@ £4 10s (£4.50)
Criggion: 1 lime wagon @ £4
Redhill: 1 6 ton truck @ £2 10s (£2.50)

One puzzling fact is that no coaches were recorded in the sales and as they had at least a scrap value their fate remains a mystery.

Action

On 19 September 1890 the Shropshire Railways formally and finally took over what remained of the old Potts. It was not much – and most of that would have to be swept away and built anew. The contract for this task was awarded to Messrs Charles Chambers of Westminster and was to be completed within 12 months. The two principal undertakings involved were the relaying of the whole of the main line to Llanymynech and the raising of Abbey station above flood level; this would also have considerably eased the gradient down into the station. The connection with the Wellington line was also to be restored, the Criggion branch more or less abandoned and the Nantmawr line left in the capable hands of the Cambrian.

For some nine months work progressed apace. Virtually the whole of the main line was cleared, fenced and resleepered, a start was made on the work at Abbey and on replacing the timber bridges with ones of more durable materials. Then, on 15 July 1891, it all stopped. Cessation of work was the result of financial complications, seemly engineered by the firm of Whadcoat Bros Ltd, debenture holders in the SR, who had been paying the contractor directly. Not all the proceedings appear to have been entirely above board; Whadcoats ceased paying Chambers while on 11 November, following a Chancery action against the SR, a Receiver was appointed and, like the reconstruction, the promotors' dreams came to an abrupt full stop.

Nantmawr branch developments

The only part of the line that seemed to have any future was the Nantmawr branch, worked by the Cambrian. That company now set about securing its hold by incorporating it fully into its general pattern of operations. On 11 April 1894 it reached an agreement with the SR's Receiver whereby it would construct a ½ mile deviation from its Llanfyllin branch to join the Nantmawr branch west of Llanymynech at Wern. Thus by using this new line and the 55 chains of the Nantmawr branch from Wern Junction to Llanymynech, CR trains for either branch could use that station's facilities. The Nantmawr branch reopened on 1 January 1896 and the deviation on 27 January 1896. The remaining section of the branch was now nothing more than an offshoot of the Llanfyllin branch. A new agreement was made on 12 April 1900 whereby the CR would formally lease it in return for the tolls it was paying; this would come into effect from 1 July, last for 99 years and guarantee a minimum return to the SR of £555 per year. At least half of this was to be paid by the CR and the remainder by the Tanat Valley Light Railway which had opened on 5 January

The wilderness encroaches: Nesscliff station (left) in 1903, looking west. (L&GRP)

1904 after decades of promotion and speculation. Authorised by the Tanat Valley Light Railway Order of 1898 this line was a westward extension of the Cambrian's Porthywaen mineral branch from the Oswestry–Welshpool main line north of Llanymynech and ran roughly parallel to the Llanfyllin branch. From the outset the line was worked by the Cambrian (and finally absorbed by it in 1921) and crossed the Nantmawr branch at Llanyblodwel. The TVLR joined the former Potts line from the east just north of the station — renamed Blodwell Junction — and departed for

Llanymynech station, 1902, with locomotive shed in background. (L&GRP)

places west just south of it. Blodwell Junction thus became in effect just another station on the TVLR; the major portion of the Nantmawr branch south from here to Wern Junction had become merely an obsolete connecting line between these two points (though the two timber viaducts had been rebuilt by the CR with concrete piers and abutments and the whole branch reballasted).

Decay

The remains of the Potts now entered their great period of dereliction. Services had been suspended in 1880, 10 years later the Shropshire Railways unsuccessfully attempted to refurbish the line but now, by the turn of the century, a further decade of

The north end of Melverley viaduct in 1893, before collapse. (*L&GRP*)

neglect had taken its toll. Many of the remains did not survive to see the later rebirth of the line; indeed, it would have been an extremely gifted onlooker who could have forseen such an improbable occurrence. With each passing year the decay advanced just that little further. Buildings slowly sagged and finally collapsed;

Richard Reeves (in waistcoat) with the maintenance trolley west of Hanwood Road. The bridge arch is the SR's replacement of a wooden structure. (*L&GRP*)

Hanwood Road, Redhill, Shrawardine and Maesbrook stations disappeared entirely. The Criggion branch virtually went the same way under a sea of encroaching vegetation while Melverley viaduct toppled and was washed away. Part of the parapet of the new Rea bridge fell off one day into the water below. Abbey station itself was converted into a stable while the trackbed between the platforms was filled in and the whole area used as a coal merchant's yard.

One man, Richard Reeves, ex-Potts guard, was

appointed by the Receiver to maintain the fences on the line and for this purpose he travelled to and from the scene of each day's work on the old hand-propelled trolley. To do anything more than keep cattle from straying down the line was an impossible task; time worked its ravages and as the physical presence of the railway began to blur and soften, so too did the memories of those who had once ridden it. A whole new generation grew up for whom it had never even existed.

Chapter 4

THE SHROPSHIRE & MONTGOMERYSHIRE LIGHT RAILWAY 1907 – 1941

Colonel H. F. Stephens. (*Colonel Stephens Railway Museum, Tenterden*)

Colonel H. F. Stephens

To any reasonable person, it might well have seemed that the railway was not only dead but buried as well – but no; local voices could still be heard demanding its resurrection and the most sympathetic ear they could find belonged to Colonel Holman Fred Stephens. In the history of the railways of these islands, Colonel Stephens stands out as one of the most extraordinary personages ever; his name is virtually – and justly – synonymous with the British light railway and for that involvement, together with his idiosyncratic methods of operation, his memory is deservedly venerated by all lovers of such lines. To all intents and purposes, Stephens collected railways in the way that another might open grocery shops.

Stephens' life has been covered in more detail elsewhere (see *Bibliography*); suffice to say here that he was born in London in 1868, the son of Frederic George Stephens, a member of the Pre-Raphaelite school. He trained as a civil engineer, joined the Metropolitan Railway in 1889 but left the following year to go 'independent' as builder and/or manager of a whole succession of minor railways, standard and narrow gauge, up and down the country; among those narrow gauge and light railways that will always be associated with him are such names as the Festiniog, the Welsh Highland, the Rye & Camber, the Ashover, the Snailbeach, the West Sussex, the Kent & East Sussex, the East Kent, the Weston, Cleveland & Portishead – and, of course, the Shropshire & Montgomeryshire.

By 1907 the Colonel – although invariably referred to by this title, Stephens was not actually awarded his rank of Lt Col in the Royal Engineers (TR) until the first world war – had his offices established in Tonbridge, Kent, and from here he managed his growing empire. An obvious and passionate believer in the effectiveness of light railways in rural areas, permitted by the 1896 Light Railways Act to promote and construct such lines cheaply, he decided to accept the challenge of resuscitating the old Potts. On 30 May 1907, an application for the relevant Light Railway Order was made to the Light Railway Commissioners. The question was, would it be a repetition of the Shropshire Railways fiasco all over again?

The Light Railway Orders

The Light Railway Commissioners' local inquiry into the application was held on 9 June at

The Potts station at Llanyblodwel, looking north, with coal office on the left. (L&GRP)

Wern Junction, 1904, looking west; the new CR Llanfyllin line is on the left; the old alignment used the demolished bridge over the Nantmawr line in the centre. (L&GRP)

Shrewsbury; no objection to the line was offered by either the GWR or the LNWR – presumably in the not unreasonable belief that the scheme was hopeless – and the application was approved. Estimated cost of reconstruction was £40,000. Before things could progress further, some sort of arrangement had to be agreed with the SR. In the

Edgebold station in S&M days, with the building and pivoted crossbar stop signal characteristic of the railway. (*Lens of Sutton*)

Chancery Division of the High Court a draft agreement between the company on one hand, and Stephens, the Earl of Bradford and William Rigby, a London contractor, on the other, was approved on 17 January 1908. Under it, the new promotors were to reconstruct the old SR, with the exception of the Nantmawr branch, as a light railway, in return for the SR being empowered to issue 4½% prior charge debentures to nominees of the new company to a total of £40,000 (one-fifth of which

Shrawardine station. The rotating stop signal can be clearly seen. (*L&GRP*)

was specifically allocated for the Criggion branch). The way was now clear for the Shropshire & Montgomeryshire Light Railway Order 1909 to be issued by the Board of Trade on 11 February of that year.

Under the Order, four lines of railway were authorised: the main Shrewsbury–Llanymynech line, the Criggion branch, the connection with the Wellington line and a connection with the joint line from Shrewsbury to Hereford. The first three were to be straightforward reconstructions of the former SR lines while the fourth was to be the construction of the spur authorised for but never built by the SR. Work was to commence within 12

Kinnerley station with stock in the Criggion branch bay on the right. (*Lens of Sutton*)

months, and be completed in 18, for the main line; the Criggion branch reconstruction had first to receive the consent of the SR and be completed eighteen months after that. All lines were to be worked by the Shropshire & Montgomeryshire Light Railway Co, newly-formed with Stephens, Rigby and the Earl of Bradford as the first three directors. Authorised capital was £2,000 in £10

shares, half of which could only be issued with the SR's consent, and promises were received of loans secured by the debenture issue totalling £5,750 made up as follows: Shropshire County Council – £2,000; Montgomeryshire County Council – £1,500; Atcham Rural District Council – £1,000; Oswestry Rural District Council – £250; Shrewsbury Corporation and Forden Rural District Council – £500 each.

On 19 March a group of local supporters paid a visit to two of Stephens' other ventures, the East Kent Light Railway and the Kent & East Sussex

The former Potts station building at Kinnerley, refurbished by the S&M. (*Photomatic*)

A scene that beautifully captures the atmosphere of the S&M at work: the locomotive shed and roads at Kinnerley with (right) *Gazelle*, trailer 16, the Ford rail-lorry and Ford railcar in front of the stray tender. (*L&GRP*)

Railway, and were apparently much impressed. It would appear however that the plans for linking the new railway with the national system at Shrewsbury were undergoing drastic revision, probably on the grounds of expense and operational convenience. In May 1909 a second application for a Light Railway Order was made. Approved without a local inquiry, it was granted as the Shropshire & Montgomeryshire Light Railway (Amendment) Order 1910, and issued by the Board of Trade on 19 July of that year. It had two main provisions relevant to the actual reconstruction: first, the Wellington line junction was now authorised at Meole Brace, nearly two miles from Shrewsbury; and second, the company was not 'prohibited from opening for public traffic the part of the railway north of the Severn River Bridge at Shrawardine prior to the opening of the remainder of the railway in the event of such part being constructed previously to the construction of the remainder'. Obviously, the intention was to commence work at the Llanymynech end of the line – and possibly obtain some revenue from it before reaching Shrewsbury!

Reconstruction

The S&M was now faced with the task of rebuilding a railway which had, in theory, already been reconstructed once. Col Stephens adopted his usual guiding policy in such instances: make do or mend – and, only if all else fails, replace. According to *The Locomotive Magazine* of 15 October 1910, work began in earnest at the end of September; the hardest part was probably hacking a way through some 30 years' growth of trees and bushes in order to get at the track. It was soon discovered that while the old Potts rails were generally in reasonable shape, the relaid (and uncreosoted) SR sleepers were not. So, working from Llanymynech, where the only rail connection with the outside world remained, some 36,000 sleepers were replaced at 3ft intervals and the track relaid with Potts rails and chairs; a few secondhand chairs were also used. The works train was headed by a Manning Wardle 0–6–0 tank.

What remained of any level crossing gates were removed and added to the bonfires; each side of the roadway cattle grids were added and warning notices erected. Bridges fared somewhat better. Generally speaking, they were found to be quite adequate; where they were not, girders from the side where the original second track had been lifted were used to strengthen the other half. The only major construction task was the rebuilding of Melverley viaduct; a new one, consisting of girders on wooden piers, was erected to the east of where the old one had been.

The stations were treated in similar fashion, usually refurbished, occasionally replaced. At the same time the opportunity was taken to add several new ones and rename some of the old. Working up the line, the new position was as follows:

Shrewsbury Abbey Foregate – the former station block was converted back into booking office, waiting room, traffic office and lavatory. The 230ft long and 10ft wide platform was on the site chosen by the SR (on a higher level than the Potts) and stood 3ft above rail level with a running

Much the same view as on the previous page but, in 1938, taken at a rather sadder time in the railway's life. (*L&GRP*)

line on each side; in addition there was a bay platform and a small goods yard.

Shrewsbury West (1 mile) – new platform halt where the S&M neared the line to Welshpool.

Meole Brace ($1\frac{3}{4}$ miles) – new station with booking office and exchange sidings with the Welshpool line.

Hookagate & Redhill (3 miles) – new station just to the east of the old Redhill.

Edgebold (4 miles) – the renamed Hanwood Road with a new building.

Cruckton ($5\frac{3}{4}$ miles) – new platform halt with shelter.

Shoot Hill ($6\frac{3}{4}$ miles) – new platform halt.

A typical S&M halt: Wern Las, 1935. (*Photomatic*)

Ford & Crossgates ($7\frac{1}{4}$ miles) – the old Ford station renamed and refurbished.

Shrawardine ($9\frac{1}{2}$ miles) – new station building added.

Nesscliff & Pentre ($11\frac{3}{4}$ miles) – the renamed Nesscliff.

Edgerley ($12\frac{1}{2}$ miles) – new platform halt.

Kinnerley ($13\frac{1}{4}$ miles) – goods yard added and the station refurbished.

Wern Las (15 miles) – new platform halt.

Maesbrook (16 miles) – new station building added.

Llanymynech (18 miles) – station refurbished. On the Criggion branch the old stations were refurbished and a new halt $\frac{3}{4}$ mile from Kinnerley – Chapel Lane – added.

From the above list of new stations and names it is easy to deduce the S&M's policy on attracting passengers: provide a stopping place at any

convenient road crossing and name it after the closest area – or preferably two areas – of habitation. Unless otherwise stated, the new halts were simple brick or wooden platforms and the new station buildings a standard wooden pattern housing a stationmaster's room, a booking office and a waiting room. Not all the halts were apparently planned from the outset; rather they were gradually added during the first few months of operations as local demands became clear, or hoped for.

Open once again

The official opening of the new railway took place on Thursday 13 April 1911, the proceedings commencing in the delightful spring mid-morning at Abbey station. Invited guests numbered some 200, the principal dignitaries being the Mayor of Shrewsbury, Major Wingfield; the Deputy Mayor, Alderman Benjamin Blower; the Chairman of Shropshire County Council, Mr J. Bowen-Jones and a host of representatives from the other various local authorities involved. Holding the borough's loving cup aloft, Major Wingfield delivered the following benediction from the roof of the first train's leading coach:

> We are assembled here to open the Shropshire and Montgomeryshire Light Railway, a railway which I trust and think will be of great benefit to this borough and to the country districts which it serves between Shrewsbury and Llanymynech. (Cheers.) It will benefit the district by bringing in the produce of the farmers; it will benefit the borough by that produce being brought into Shrewsbury and sold in the borough. (Hear, hear and applause.) Therefore it is a kind of mutual benefit railway which I have the honour of opening today. (Cheers.) I hear the engine blowing off steam, so for fear it should burst I curtail my remarks and drink out of the loving cup "Success to the Shropshire and Montgomeryshire Light Railway". (Cheers.)
>
> (*The Shrewsbury Chronicle* 21 April 1911)

The guests boarded the waiting train without further ado and, to the cheers of the inevitable crowd and to the equally inevitable fusilade of fog signals, *Hesperus* pulled out at the head of four coaches, two brakevans and a pair of Cambrian saloon carriages borrowed especially for the occasion. (One of these had borne no less a personage than King Edward VII himself on a trip over the Birmingham Waterworks Railway at Rhayader seven years earlier.) Past the cheering,

flag-waving crowds ran the train, running (in the words of *The Shrewsbury Chronicle*), 'with a smoothness which would not compare unfavourably with some of the greater railways of the country'.

The first halt came at Hookagate & Redhill where the passengers disembarked to be duly recorded by the camera of Councillor R. L. Bartlett; the second was at Kinnerley where 82 year-old Richard Reeves welcomed the train in a uniform which had hung unused for so many years. Then all the way on to Llanymynech, steaming in to more cheers and fog signals. Here the party was greeted by the Chairman of Llanymynech Parish Council, Mr J. Kemble, before taking a half hour break for sandwiches, during which interval the loving cup was put to good use! The return journey was made minus the two Cambrian coaches and was uninterrupted save for a short stop at Kinnerley where the new locomotive shed and the Criggion branch junction were inspected. Shrewsbury was safely reached at approximately 3.30pm.

'Safely' was, unfortunately, not a word to remain linked with the S&M for long. Although the next day, Good Friday, the first day of public services, passed without incident, the Saturday was marred by a derailment on the Shrewsbury side of Hookagate & Redhill. The train involved was due at Abbey Foregate to form the 6.45pm back to Llanymynech but failed to arrive, the explanation being that upon rounding a sharp curve beyond the station *Hesperus*, travelling tender-first, became derailed. The end result was engine and three coaches off the rails, tender (!) and two coaches on them and a long stretch of damaged track. Incredibly, no-one seems to have been injured, helped no doubt by the fact that all parts of the train managed to remain upright on top of the embankment. Under Stephens' direction, and aided by the LNWR breakdown crane and gang from Shrewsbury, the railway staff worked right through until Sunday afternoon to repair the damage – watched of course by the inevitable crowds!

Just four days later the incident was repeated, the train this time being the 1.25pm from Shrewsbury which came off the rails at Maesbrook. Fortunately the repetition extended to cover the escape of the passengers and the damage was made good the following day. In all it must have been an extremely disquieting time for both the local residents and the directors of the

Hesperus after the derailment at Redhill, Easter 1911. (*L&GRP*)

company, coming so soon after the Board of Trade inspection. In the phrase of *The Shrewsbury Chronicle*, the interval between inspection and accidents had been 'amazingly short'. Although still very much in support of the railway, and full of sympathy for, and faith in, its directors, the paper pointed out that to avoid being crushed like the Potts by an overwhelming burden of capital expenditure, the construction of the line had been undertaken as cheaply as possible. In view of the railway's subsequent record, though, it appears to have been a case of simply not bedding in the track adequately, an omission that was soon naturally put right. Newly relaid track needs several weeks to consolidate with low spots being packed up.

All that remained was for the Criggion branch to open and the railway would be fully in business; this it did in February 1912 for goods, and for passengers in August of the same year. The S&M now settled down to what was to be the most unchanging period of its life, for during the next 30-odd years nothing of spectacular note really happened. New (ie secondhand) engines and items of rolling stock were occasionally purchased by the Colonel; full details are given in the following two chapters. Of special interest was the experiment with railcars in the 1920s, an experiment not greeted with enthusiasm by those forced to ride in them!

In all, the S&M was very much the epitome of a Stephens railway: of light construction, equipped with antiquated and ill-matching stock serving rural halts miles from anywhere. The potential passenger traffic was little enough to begin with; when the motor car and bus began to nibble away at it, the line's future became increasingly unclear.

The post-Colonel years

The Stephens empire, for all its astonishing diversity, was very much a one-man business and,

Shropshire & Montgomeryshire Railway.

SUPPORT THE LOCAL LINE.

THIS Line runs through a delightful country and affords the travelling public every possible facility for pleasure and trading. There are numerous sites adjacent to the railway system suitable for the erection of works and factories of every description.

A Service of
RAIL MOTOR CARS
is now running between
SHREWSBURY, FORD, LLANYMYNECH & KINNERLEY.

CHEAP EXCURSIONS
are run from Shrewsbury to Llanymynech for
GOLF LINKS,
and Fishing in the River Vyrnwy thereon and to Criggion for the
BRIEDDEN HILLS.

CHEAP DAY EXCURSIONS
TO
CRIGGION AND LLANYMYNECH.

Five large Camping Huts adjoining the River Severn, near Crew Green Station, have been provided, and Rowing Boats are to be hired at cheap rates.
The attractions are—Fishing, Rowing, Boating, and Bathing. Sketching and Hill Climbing, only half a mile from the Briedden Hills.
Camping Huts, 7/- per week per hut, and Weekly Season Tickets, Third Class, to Salop at low rates. 10/- deposit on key of hut. Apply to Mr. John Turner, District Traffic Agent, S. & M.R., Crewe Green, Ford, or to J. L White, Abbey Station.

H. F. STEPHENS, *Managing Director.*

SUPPORT THE LOCAL LINE.

when that one man died on 23 October 1931, the whole structure began to fall apart. His friend and partner, W. H. Austen, who had been with him since he first set up on his own, took control after Stephens' death and had the unenviable task of seeing it all collapse. To say this is in no way to lay the blame on Austen; it is hard to imagine that even the Colonel's undoubted genius, had he lived, could have kept his railways going through the compound problems of the second world war, nationalisation and the increasing dominance of the road vehicle for both passenger and freight transport. This last had already showed its effect on passenger receipts during the Colonel's life.

In October 1932 passenger workings on the branch ceased beyond Melverley, ostensibly out of concern for the safety of the viaduct. Just over 12 months later, on 6 November 1933, regular passenger services over the rest of the S&M line ceased. From then on excursions were run only on special occasions, such as Bank Holidays, but even this facility was withdrawn three years later. After that, very infrequent enthusiasts' charter trains, coal and freight to intermediate stations, and the once-weekly stone train from Criggion was all the traffic the line saw.

The effects of this run-down on the general appearance of the railway quickly became apparent. Stations were closed even to freight, one by one, throughout the 1930s and left to decay; only one engine was ever kept in working order while the rest, for the most part, rusted gently away; everywhere the weeds grew. The S&M was

all but a ghost railway, just as the Potts had been, littered with deserted halts and buildings, stranded stock and obsolete pieces of locomotives whose precise origins were shrouded in mystery.

And yet, contrary to all expectations, but perfectly faithful to its incredible past, the railway's most astonishing transformation was still to come.

Working

Trains on the S&M were nothing but slow; the journey from Shrewsbury to Llanymynech took an hour by passenger train and in later years up to a quarter of an hour longer. Strictly speaking, there were no purely passenger trains as such for mixed working was the rule. To the restriction of a 25mph speed limit imposed by the Light Railway Order of 1909 (15mph for engines travelling tender first) were added all the time-consuming shunting activities this entailed at various stations along the line. The basic service changed but little over the years; usually three or four trains ran each way on the main line, increased to five on Thursdays and Saturdays and cut to two on Sundays. The Criggion branch saw three each way during the week and one on Sundays. By the late 1920s, with falling receipts, the branch service was gradually cut, first to two a day and then to Saturdays only from September 1928. By the end of passenger working in 1933 there were just two round trips over the main line on weekdays, three on Saturdays and none on Sundays.

Fares, as permitted under the 1909 Order, were 3d, 2d and 1d per mile for first, second, and third class passengers respectively, with a minimum for

The slightly (!) misleading nameboard at Wern Las. (*Photomatic*)

Llanymynech station with the end of the S&M platform in the left foreground; centre is the line to Welshpool and right the branch to Llanfyllin and Nantmawr. (*L&GRP*)

three miles. Curiously, for carrying a passenger across the River Severn, the Company was entitled to 'take an extra charge as for two additional miles' – a practice allowed to some of the main line railways where additional mileage could be charged along such major structures as the Forth bridge or Severn tunnel. Tickets were of the Edmondson type. Parcels, when carried, were marked with special labels, as were letters, with stamps of various types and surcharges being issued from 2d in 1914 to 4d in 1940.

The railway's operational centre was at Kinnerley and here, just off the Criggion branch,

Llanymynech station building, 1960. (*Photomatic*)

were the locomotive shed and shops. The station itself was on the main line and boasted two platforms and a bay for the Criggion trains; the branch was worked on the 'one engine in steam' principle. Llanymynech to Kinnerley was worked on the staff and ticket system, Kinnerley to Ford by electric tablet and from Ford to Shrewsbury by staff and ticket. All stations were connected by telegraph, with signals, worked from ground frames, at the passing places of Ford and Kinnerley, as well as at the termini and also Meole Brace. At minor halts trains were signalled to stop by a diamond-shaped board, mounted on a post, which could be swung round to face oncoming trains. It was painted red with a white stripe and showed a red light in the stop position and green for clear. Points not protected by signals were worked by an Annett's key on the train staff. Level

crossings were ungated and protected by cattle grids across the line on each side of the roadway, and had a 10mph rail speed limit.

The Nantmawr branch continued

Meanwhile the Cambrian still worked the former Nantmawr branch, but by a supplementary agreement dated 30 December 1916 the CR's payment to the SR — which remained in existence to collect it — was increased to £705 per year. After the 1923 Grouping the rent was paid by the GWR and from 1 September 1939 it rose to £886. The SR and S&M remained independent at Grouping.

By this time further major changes had taken place on what was left of the Nantmawr line. From the beginning of 1917 passenger services between Blodwell Junction and Llanymynech ceased and in 1925 goods workings over this stretch were terminated. By 1930 the northern half of the Blodwell Junction to Wern Junction section had been lifted; the southern half lasted a little longer, being lifted between 1936 and 1938.

Chapter 5

S&M LOCOMOTIVES

Col Stephens' policy of acquiring secondhand locomotives at bargain prices for his railways bore its finest fruits on the S&M. If not for anything else, the line will always be remembered for the amazing assortment of engines with which it was cluttered. These are described individually in detail below in two main groups: the S&M named series and the unnamed stock.

The named series

1 Gazelle

If the S&M typified the railways of Col Stephens, then without doubt *Gazelle* personified the S&M. It can only be described as unique. Constructed as a 2–2–2 well tank in 1893 by Alfred Dodman & Co of Highgate Works, King's Lynn, to the order of William Burkitt, twice mayor of Lynn, *Gazelle* was used in a most peculiar way. Burkitt was on very good terms with the directors and officials of the GER and the Midland & Great

Gazelle, as built. (*Photomatic*)

Gazelle, 1926. (*H. C. Casserley*)

Northern Joint, the two railways serving Lynn, and he had the locomotive built for his own personal use over their lines on his business as a seed and corn dealer. On these trips it would be in the charge of a driver from one of the main line companies and it is reported that it once ventured, on 25 July 1897, as far as Chesterfield.

Gazelle and trailer No 16 at Kinnerley, 1926. Note the ground frame on the left. (*H. C. Casserley*)

To call *Gazelle* diminutive is almost to make an understatement, as these dimensions show:

Wheel diameter: driving		3ft 9in
: trailing		2ft 3in
Total wheelbase		10ft 6in
Cylinders: diameter		4in
: stroke		12in
Overall length		17ft 9in
Overall height		7ft 9in
Weight in working order		5 tons 6cwt

In short, it had a very good claim to the title of the

Gazelle, looking as good as she has ever done, in the National Railway Museum, York, in 1980. The rear 'passenger accommodation' is no more.

smallest standard gauge locomotive in the world.

Almost everything about its design, the responsibility for which can be laid at the door of Mr S. Stone of the GER's Locomotive Department, was peculiar. All the wheels were of wood, the motion from the inside cylinders passed on each side of the firebox to the driving axle and, to crown it all, a bench seat above the bunker at the rear of the open cab provided accommodation for four passengers!

At an unknown date *Gazelle* ceased its East Anglian wanderings — no doubt because of a stricter official policy in such matters — and was

Gazelle and trailer in Kinnerley goods yard, again in 1926. (*H. C. Casserley*)

sold in 1910 to Mr T. W. Ward, a dealer, of Sheffield from whom Stephens purchased it in February 1911. The intention was to use it as an inspection locomotive and it was sent to W. G. Bagnall Ltd of Stafford and became an 0–4–2 by the replacement of the leading wheels with a second pair of drivers. Or not exactly, for what actually happened was this: the original drivers were discarded, the leading wheels were removed and one used as a pattern for four cast-iron wheels which were fitted to the original leading and driving axles, thus giving much smaller driving wheels than before, and the rebuild was completed by the addition of a pair of light coupling rods. *Gazelle* returned to Kinnerley in July 1911 but was soon returned to Bagnall for the installation of a cab covering the bunker seat. (Possibly this was not actually carried out until 1913.)

With the opening of the Criggion branch to passengers in 1912 *Gazelle* was used — without a coach! — for the conveyance of passengers, a state of affairs which prompted the vicar of Criggion, the Rev R. Brock, to complain to the Board of Trade in no uncertain terms; the Board rebuked Stephens whereupon he purchased the ex-London tramcar that became *Gazelle*'s trailer. (See Chapter 6.) With the reduction of the branch traffic it was more or less withdrawn, except for the occasional outing, and by the 1930s was stored in an increasingly-decrepit condition behind the water tower at Kinnerley. However, in June 1937 it was restored to its former glory for inspection work and private charter, coupled with a new trailer. Withdrawn from service in 1945, *Gazelle* was sent to the Longmoor Military Railway in June 1950 for preservation and there it remained until the depot closed in 1970; after display at the

Gazelle, derelict in 1935. (*L&GRP*)

National Railway Museum it went in 1981 to the Army Transport Museum at Leconfield.

2 *Hecate/Severn*

The origins of this unusual locomotive are, unfortunately, shrouded in mystery. It is believed to have originated as an 0–4–0 tender locomotive built by Bury, Curtis & Kennedy of Liverpool for

Gazelle's plates, 1980.

the Shrewsbury & Hereford Railway. From here it passed to the LNWR and then, in 1871 (when nearly 30 years old) to the Griff Colliery Co where it was converted to an 0–4–2 saddle tank and named *Crewe*. Stephens bought it in September 1911 and had it overhauled by Bagnalls, renaming it *Hecate*. Its normal duties were Criggion branch workings until withdrawn in 1931 (and scrapped 1937). From 1916 it carried the name *Severn*.

3 *Hesperus*

Hesperus was the first of three similar locomotives purchased by Stephens for the S&M. It was one of the LSWR's 0–6–0 Ilfracombe Goods or 282 Class, built to the design of W. G. Beattie by Beyer Peacock of Manchester. (Eight in all were constructed and, such was their value for light railway work – they were designed for the steeply-graded Ilfracombe branch – that Stephens eventually acquired six for his various lines.) They were inside cylinder tender engines, originally fitted with leather leading buffers, four-wheeled tenders and wooden brake shoes. From 1888 onwards all were rebuilt with slightly larger wheels, stovepipe chimneys, metal buffers and brake shoes, larger boilers and cabs and six-wheeled tenders taken from a variety of older locomotives. As rebuilt, driving wheel diameter was 4ft 7½in and the cylinders 16in x 20in.

Works No 1517, No 3 was numbered 324 by the LSWR and withdrawn in August 1910. In January 1911 it was sold to Stephens for £700; he

No 2 *Severn* standing idle at Kinnerley in 1926. (*H. C. Casserley*)

fitted it with vacuum brakes and steam heating gear and painted it in the S&M's olive green livery. It handled the bulk of the railway's passenger trains in the early years and was overhauled at Crewe in 1919. In the 1920s it was placed in store until about 1934 when it was put back into service. In June 1938 it was overhauled for the last time; in November 1941 it was cut up at Abbey Foregate.

4 *Morous*
A Manning Wardle 0–6–0 saddle tank of 1866

No 2 *Severn* in Kinnerley shed, next to an 'Ilfracombe Goods' under repair. (*Lens of Sutton*)

vintage (works No 178), *Morous* began life as a contractor's locomotive and as such was used by T. B. Crampton on the construction of the East & West Junction Railway (later the Stratford-on-Avon & Midland Junction Railway). After the opening of this line it stayed on as E&WJR No 1, was rebuilt in 1896 and became S&MJR No 1 in 1909. It was an inside cylinder engine and generally similar in design to the Manning Wardle contractor's locomotives used on the building of the Potts.

Morous was purchased (and named) by Stephens in 1910 but was found to be slightly underpowered for the line and was transferred to another of his railways, the West Sussex, in 1924.

No 3 *Hesperus*, also idle at Kinnerley. (*Lens of Sutton*)

It survived that line's closure in 1935 only to be cut up the following year. Livery was dark red, lined out in yellow and black, wheel diameter 3ft 2in and the cylinders 11in x 18in.

4 *Walton Park*

The S&M was briefly the possessor of a second No 4, again an 0–6–0 saddle tank. This was Hudswell Clarke 823 of 1908 with 3ft 7in wheels and 14in x 20in outside cylinders. It had originally been owned by the Weston, Clevedon & Portishead Railway where Stephens was Traffic Manager (Walton Park was a station on this line)

No 4 *Morous*, minus coupling rods, at Kinnerley in 1922. (*Photomatic*)

and was transferred to the S&M in 1913. In August 1916 he moved it again, this time to his East Kent Railway where it became No 2. It was sold from there in 1943 to T. W. Ward of Sheffield and wound up as *Churchill* of the Purfleet Deep Water Wharf & Storage Co in 1947.

5 *Pyramus* and 6 *Thisbe* (the first)

These two 0–6–2 side tanks were the only engines ever bought new for the S&M; moreover, they were constructed to Stephens' own design by Hawthorn Leslie in 1911 as their Nos 2878 and 2879. Driving wheels were 3ft 6in in diameter and the trailing wheels 2ft 6in; the outside cylinders were 14in x 16in. Unfortunately, at 36 tons they proved too heavy for the permanent way (which, after all, was only ballasted with earth) and both

No 6 *Thisbe*, the second, at Kinnerley in 1926. (*H. C. Casserley*)

were sold at the end of 1914 to the Woolmer Instructional (later Longmoor) Military Railway. There they became War Department Nos 84 and 85, though there is some uncertainty as to which engine took which number.

5 *Pyramus* and 6 *Thisbe* (the second)

The names and numbers of the above two engines were given, after their withdrawal, to the other two Ilfracombe Goods 0–6–0s purchased by Stephens. No 5 was Beyer Peacock works No 1428 of 1874, rebuilt 1890, and formerly LSWR

No 8 *Dido* in service, 1926. (*H. C. Casserley*)

No 300. It was bought for the S&M in November 1914, withdrawn in the late 1920s and cut up in 1932. No 6 was works No 1209 of 1873, LSWR No 283, rebuilt 1888 and also withdrawn by the LSWR in January 1914. It was bought by Stephens in May 1916, repainted blue with red lining like No 5 and similarly fitted with vacuum brake equipment. In 1932 it received No 5's boiler in accordance of Stephens' traditional policy of cannibalism wherever possible, but was withdrawn three years later and scrapped in 1937.

7 *Hecate,* 8 *Dido* and 9 *Daphne*

All these three engines were LBSCR Terriers (A1 class) 0–6–0 tanks with 4ft 5½in wheels and

No 9 *Daphne* at Kinnerley, 1926; the chimney of *Severn* on the right. (*H. C. Casserley*)

17in x 24in inside cylinders. Originally Nos 81 *Beulah* of 1880, 38 *Millwall* of 1878 and 83 *Earlswood* of 1880 respectively, they were bought by Stephens from military installations in Scotland in August 1921 (No 7) and November 1923 (Nos 8 and 9). They were not apparently a great success on the S&M – none of the tank engines seemed to be – and were withdrawn during the early 1930s; Nos 7 and 8 were dismantled and used for spare parts for servicing the Terriers on other Stephens lines. *Daphne* was purchased by the Southern Railway in December 1938 for a similar purpose.

The unnamed locomotives

By 1930 it was clear that replacements were needed for the ageing Ilfracombe Goods and in the March of that year an ex-LNWR 0–6–0 was

LNW 0–6–0 No 8108, on a train at Shrewsbury Abbey, before its overhaul. (*Lens of Sutton*)

purchased from the LMS. Built in 1874 it had been LMS No 8108 and was followed in 1931 and 1932 by two similar engines, Nos 8182 of 1879 and 8236 of 1881. All had 4ft 3in driving wheels and 17in x 24in inside cylinders. Scarcely younger than the Ilfracombe Goods, they coped well, nevertheless, with their not too demanding duties on the S&M. Towards the end of the decade No 8108 underwent some eighteen months' repairs, emerging from Kinnerley workshops in May 1939 freshly-painted in green similar to Southern olive green and numbered 2. The new image, alas, was not destined to last, for under the War Department, which was shortly to take over the line, it reverted to its old number and was repainted in camouflage green. Its two companions also received the latter treatment, putting paid to plans to renumber them 4 and 5 to complete the sequence from 1 *Gazelle* and 3 *Hesperus*. All three were withdrawn in 1946 and left at Hookagate until removal to Swindon for scrapping in 1950.

Two of the LNW 0–6–0s on shed, ready for their not too arduous duties. (*Photomatic*)

Chapter 6

S&M ROLLING STOCK

The railcars

The S&M operated three sets of railcar units, two powered by Ford motors and the other by Wolseley-Siddeley engines. The S&M was not the only line on which Stephens experimented with railcars; while on the S&M the venture was only a qualified success at best he used similar vehicles on his Kent & East Sussex and West Sussex railways.

The three-car Ford railbus

This unit was constructed by the Thetford firm of Messrs Edmunds in 1923 especially for the S&M and consisted of two motor vehicles and an unpowered middle car. The motor vehicles resembled nothing less than motor buses mounted on flanged wheels, which was scarcely surprising considering the fact that they were just light bus bodies on bus chassis, complete with bonnet, radiator, mudguards and headlamps at the front (though the steering gear was removed)! The centre car was a matching vehicle, coupled to the others with drawpin connections; all three ran on four 2ft 6in diameter pressed-steel wheels with inside bearings on solid axles. Each car measured 17ft 4in in length and the motor vehicles seated 19 passengers each and the centre car 24 on bus-type seats. All cars were fitted with a roof rail around the edge of the roof for the conveyance of luggage. Access was by side doors to the motor cars and from there by sliding end doors to the centre car. Livery was blue.

Details of trials carried out on the S&M were reported in the *Locomotive Magazine* for 1923. Laden with bags of coal to equal a full complement of passengers, the three-car set ran for 50 miles on 7 gallons of petrol; working as a two-car unit petrol consumption improved substantially to $1\frac{1}{2}$ gallons for 18 miles. It was also claimed that gradients of 1 in 50 could be tackled for short distances and 1 in 130 could be climbed for long stretches without overheating. In actual service full complements of passengers were rarely, if ever, carried, and fuel consumption averaged out at roughly 14mpg. Average working speed was 25mph but top speed was slightly higher. When running, the rear motor car transmission was placed in neutral and the unit was driven and powered from the front car. There was no form of multiple working of the two motor vehicles as we know today with diesel trains.

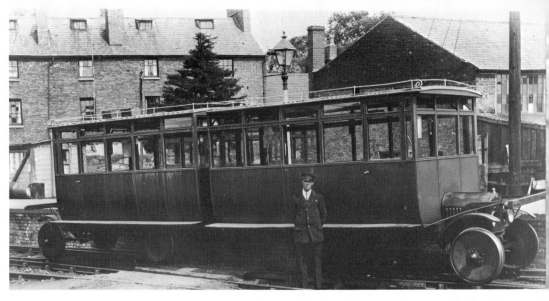

The Ford railcars, running as a two-car set, at Shrewsbury Abbey. (*Lens of Sutton*)

The set was withdrawn at an unknown date during the 1930s and survived in a derelict condition until scrapped in 1941.

The two-car Wolseley-Siddeley

Constructed during 1923 this unit was ordered and purchased in that year from Edmunds but operated only until 1929. It quickly became derelict and was scrapped c1935 though several of the seats were salvaged and used on station platforms. It is believed that one car of this unit was saved and converted into a trailer for *Gazelle* in 1937. Little is known about the constructional details of these cars other than that each had a

The Ford railcars at Llanymynech with rather more passengers this time. (*L&GRP*)

Wolseley-Siddeley engine with chain drive to the wheels. In appearance the cars had an overall resemblance to the three-car Ford set though they usually ran with an open wagon in the centre for light goods and parcels.

The single-car Ford

This was an unusual vehicle, a 'goods railcar' consisting of a chassis and cab on four pressed steel wheels. Constructed sometime between 1919 and 1925, it had a Ford engine and cab and was matched up in operation with a motor vehicle from one of the other sets to form a mixed unit. Unfortunately no other details survive of this diminutive oddity.

As can be seen from the withdrawal dates the railcars were not in service for any length of time. Although they were convenient to operate and cheap to run, they were a product of the pioneer

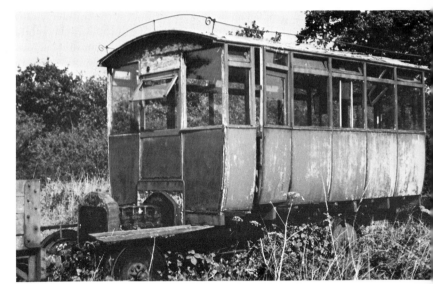

One of the Wolseley–Siddeley railcars derelict at Kinnerley (its mate became the new trailer for *Gazelle*) in 1936. Note the different cant of the roof from the Ford cars. (*Photomatic*)

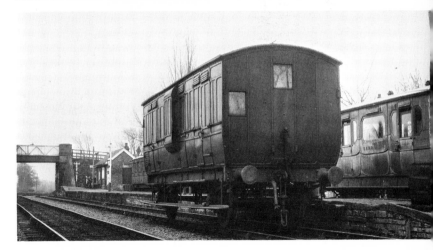

Coach No 1, ex-MR, at Kinnerley, 1935. (*Photomatic*)

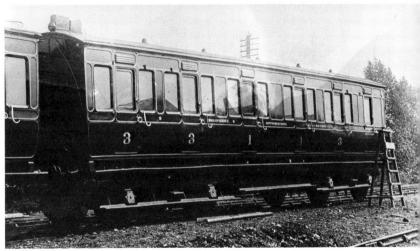

Coach No 6, also ex-MR, in its early years on the S&M. (*L&GRP*)

period of railcar development before successful designs had emerged on some of the main line railways in Britain and Ireland in the 1930s. All suffered badly from lack of adhesion and in wet weather had great difficulty in tackling the bank out of Abbey Station. Moreover they lacked sufficient power to haul trailing vehicles, bearing in mind that the equivalent road bus of similar type had only itself to move.

Passenger stock

One of the features of the S&M was the number of passenger vehicles for which it provided a home. Stephens could never seriously have thought that they might all be needed at once; like his engines they were picked up in job lots or as one-off bargains and many were destined simply to stand in the rain and rot between occasional raids for spare parts. As a result any match between the official returns and the number of vehicles actually in service at any one time was purely coincidental. Details are given of all the stock known to have been on the line during the Stephens era in order of their arrival; fuller accounts are reserved for the more interesting items. Livery was ultramarine with vermilion ends; later this was changed to buff.

1 & 2
These were a pair of ex-Midland Railway brake vans purchased in 1911 and scrapped c1950; No 2 is believed to have ended its life as a platelayers' cabin.

3 & 4
Also ex-MR, these were a pair of compartment third class bogie coaches. Also arriving in 1911, they were scrapped c1948.

5 & 6
The last of the ex-MR 1911 stock, No 5 was a bogie brake third and No 6 a bogie first/third brake composite. Both were scrapped c1948.

7 – 12
These six coaches were acquired from the Plymouth, Devonport & South Western Junction Railway and made up the rest of the railway's original stock. All were four-wheeled vehicles, ex-LSWR, and consisted of three compartment thirds, one first/third composite and two brake thirds. One of the latter was No 12; the exact numbering of the others of this batch is uncertain.

13 – 15
These were three ex-North Staffordshire Railway vehicles, again all four-wheelers, bought c1916. No 14 was a first/third composite while the other two were third class only.

16
The first passenger vehicle bought for use with *Gazelle* had as unlikely an origin as that locomotive. Purchased in 1916, it was a double-deck tramcar originally drawn by two horses in London! Conversion for the S&M's requirements consisted of removing the two end platforms, stairways, top seats, rails and decency boards, fitting four minuscule wheels together with railway running and buffing gear, and making minor alterations to the bodywork. These latter included a new roof over the old top deck, sliding doors with steps below them on each end and a large lamp housing on diagonally opposite corners. A hand operated horizontal wheel at one end provided a chain worked braking system. Inside, a longitudinal seat ran along each side.

Overall dimensions were approximately 16ft long by 6ft 6in wide; the wheels were about 1ft 6in in diameter. The carriage was awarded the stock number of 16 and carried the legend S & MR in large (later small) letters on each side below the centre window and the number below the right hand end side window. During the early 1930s it was withdrawn along with *Gazelle* and left to rot in a siding behind Kinnerley shed. The rotting process was successful as far as the body was concerned but the mechanical gear was salvaged for use on the second trailer (see below).

17
This was a four-wheeled brake third, arriving c1919 from the Kent & East Sussex Railway. Originally it had come from the GER and was scrapped in 1952.

18
Acquired in 1921 from the North London Railway, this was a four-wheeled brake van, also scrapped in 1952.

1A
With its combination of age and origin, pride of place must surely go to No 1A. Also obtained from the Plymouth, Devonport & South Western Junction Railway, this venerable coach also began life as an LSWR vehicle. Its pedigree was however

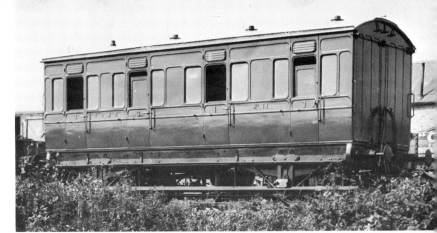

Coach No 14, ex-North Staffordshire Railway, in 1926. (*H. C. Casserley*)

S&M coach No 3, an all-third built by the Midland in the 1870s. (*L&GRP*)

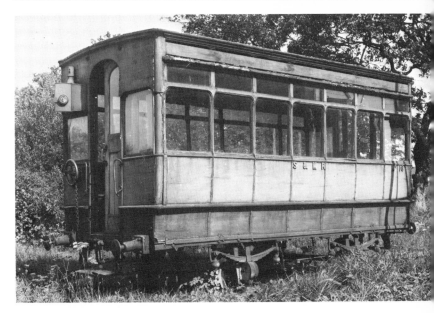

Gazelle's trailer No 16, the ex-LCC tramcar, derelict at Kinnerley. (*Lens of Sutton*)

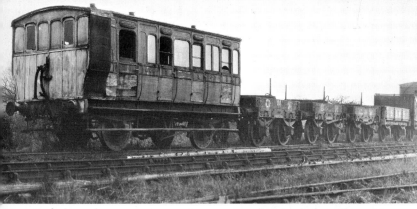

Coach No 17, originally ex-Great Eastern, at Kinnerley in 1935. (*Photomatic*)

Coach No 1A, the former LSWR royal saloon, after withdrawal. (*L&GRP*)

somewhat more exalted than its fellows as it was built in 1848 as part of the LSWR royal train. Three coaches of the set were later acquired by the PD&SWJR; two were bought by Stephens for use on the Kent & East Sussex and the S&M. The one destined for the latter line was painted blue, a livery it retained throughout its life, and arrived c1926.

No 1A was a tiny four-wheeled saloon with two doors on each side and a full-length running board beneath them. Both ends were glazed and, a reminder of its intended service, it was altogether a very comfortable and gracious vehicle to ride in. By 1953, then an incredible 105 years old, it had been relegated to the breakdown train; in the December of that year it was sent to the Longmoor Military Railway. It was to prove the veteran's last journey, for scrapping took place there in 1957. Preservation was alas found to be impossible, despite the growing impetus of preservation at that time, for it was well rotted and badly eaten away with woodworm.

Gazelle's second trailer

When *Gazelle* was resurrected in 1937 a new trailer had to be found for it and the choice, as far as can be ascertained, fell upon one of the Wolseley-Siddeley cars which, with the engine, bonnet and wheels removed was mounted upon the running gear salvaged from No 16 (though with a lengthened wheelbase of about 8ft). The former side doors were sealed up and new entrances provided via steps and sliding doors at each end. Livery was dark green with S & MR in small white letters below the centre windows. Overall width was 7ft 6½in and length over buffer beams 13ft 8½in. The trailer was never awarded a number and was withdrawn just two years later, in 1939; the body was in later years used as a hut at Kinnerley.

Goods stock

Like the passenger vehicles, all the goods stock too appears to have been secondhand and totalled some 50 wagons in all, including at least one horse box and six cattle trucks. Most, though, were probably never used on a regular basis and soon found themselves quietly crumbling away on a siding somewhere; the Criggion stone traffic was carried in the quarry company's own wagons. Possibly the most useful was the 5ton travelling crane (hand operated) used in the breakdown train. Rather unusually, no guards vans were ever used, the rear wagon carrying a 'last vehicle' indicator instead.

A rake of assorted passenger vehicles at Kinnerley in 1938.
(*L&GRP*)

Chapter 7

LAST LEASE OF LIFE 1941 – 1960

A military operation

In 1941 the S&M was requisitioned by the War Department, almost in its entirety – property, main line and stock. All that was excluded from the takeover was the Criggion branch; from then on the stone traffic was slotted into the military timetable, as was a daily civilian goods working over the main line. The purpose of the requisition was to develop the railway to feed a massive system of stores laid out in the flat surrounding countryside; such rural outposts were deliberately chosen to minimise the risks of bomb damage. With the railway the WD took over the five surviving locomotives, the coaches, one luggage and parcels van, 17 wagons and a crane.

With typical military thoroughness the line was reconstructed from end to end. Most of the old wooden sleepers were replaced with concrete sleepers, new 75lb flat bottom rails were laid and the whole ballasted properly. In the surrounding 23 square miles of requisitioned land, ammunition and other dumps were established and branches or spurs put in to the main line; Hookagate & Redhill station was removed and extensive exchange sidings laid to connect with the Welshpool line; extra sidings and loops were added or lifted elsewhere as necessary. Military passenger halts – simple concrete platforms – were built to serve at Ford, Shrawardine, Pentre, Nesscliff and Kinnerley and a new, four-platformed station, known as Lonsdale, was constructed on a branch serving the camp at Nesscliff.

Run by the No 1 Railway Group of the Royal Engineers, the S&M was now very much a military concern, both as a working railway and as a means of teaching army operating practices. From 1 June 1941 until his death in 1947, overall control was in the hands of W. Proctor, and then assumed by C. H. Calder. Locomotive stock at the time of the takeover consisted of *Gazelle, Hesperus* and the three LNWR 0–6–0s; these were replaced by a wide variety of WD locomotives and railcars, with most of the workings being handled by ex-GWR Dean Goods 0–6–0s. Comprehensive details of all the WD motive power can be found in E. S. Tonks' account of the line (see *Bibliography*), together with full accounts of the military operation of the railway.

The Criggion branch however retained the old flavour and appearance of the S&M to the last, even to the extent that when in 1945 Melverley viaduct showed signs of imminent collapse, a typical S&M solution was found: the British

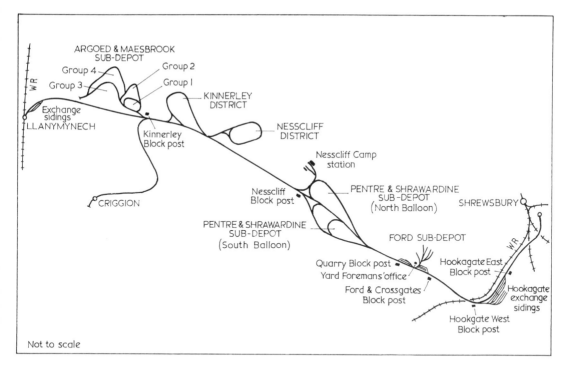

Not to scale

Quarrying Co's Sentinel locomotive (No 7026) pushed the daily stone train cautiously over the sagging structure to be collected on the other side by the S&M engine. Eventually it was thought that this arrangement was too laborious and the vertical-boilered shunter toiled all the way to Kinnerley with the wagons at its top speed of 5mph! In 1948 work was begun by a Reading firm of contractors, Messrs A. E. Farr Ltd, on the erection of a new viaduct just upstream from the old one.

Post-war run-down

As with so many things, the end of the war in 1945 did not signal an immediate return to normality and it was not until 1947 that the S&M was assigned WD Civilian rather than Military status. The following year came nationalisation when BR stock was distributed to S&M shareholders at the current market rate for their shares: 6d (2½p) per £10 − a value of only £25 for the whole railway which was slightly at odds with the estimated scrap value of £32,696 made up thus:

Permanent way	£27,424
Property	£4,050
Rolling stock	£622
Station buildings	£600

In many respects, the S&M fared extremely well during the war years; so too did its traffic figures with the wartime preference for rail rather than road transport (and the construction of the stores and dumps):

Year	Public tonnage	WD tonnage
1939	35,574	—
1940	20,984	—
1941	122,525	—
1942	49,150	209,216
1943	40,452	349,986
1944	46,959	295,593
1945	43,901	146,330
1946	41,736	38,563
1947	40,910	31,601

The WD gradually ran-down its operations, disposing of surplus stock and slowly closing the sub-depots one by one; in 1954 the siding laid into the new milk factory at Edgebold, opened in 1942, was lifted.

In 1959 matters came to a head. The WD closed its last sub-depots and lifted its last branches while in December of that year the stone traffic from Criggion ceased. The last scheduled train ran over the main line on 26 February 1960 and on 29 February the line officially closed; on 20 March a farewell trip was made over the railway by the Stephenson Locomotive Society. BR put in a new connection to the line, this time from the end of the closed Severn Valley line to Abbey goods yard,

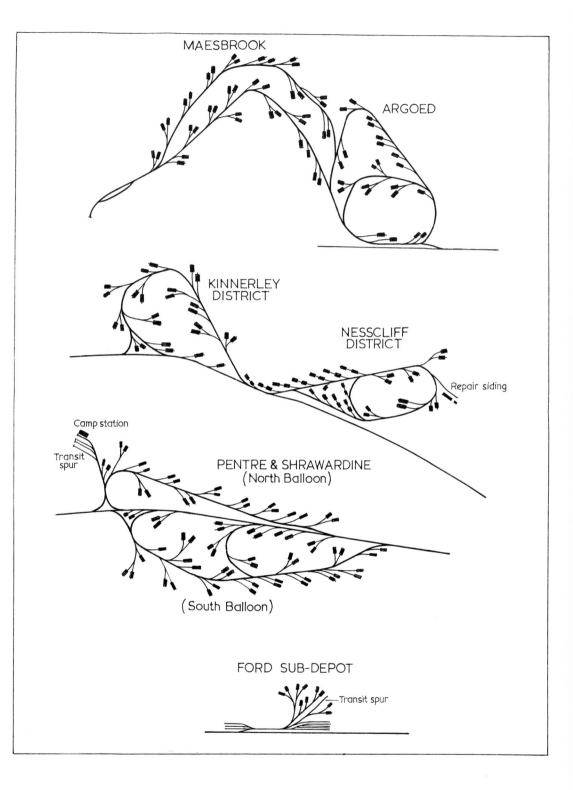

MAESBROOK

ARGOED

KINNERLEY
DISTRICT

NESSCLIFF
DISTRICT

Repair siding

Camp station

Transit
spur

PENTRE & SHRAWARDINE
(North Balloon)

(South Balloon)

FORD SUB-DEPOT

Transit spur

WD Austerity 0–6–0STs Nos 188 and 193 at Kinnerley, 20 March 1960. (*Photomatic*)

which it wished to retain, and on 31 March the old S&M was formally handed over to BR by the WD for disposal.

And once again — goodbye

The first part of the railway to go was the Criggion branch then, in 1962, the main line was lifted with the exception of Hookagate exchange sidings and Abbey goods yard, now used as a permanent way

WD 193 with the Stephenson Locomotive Society special, 20 March 1960. Although hardly distinguishable, the back coach is one of the LTSR Ealing–Southend train vehicles of pre first world war build. (*Photomatic*)

The end of the truncated Severn Valley line. Centre is the line to Shrewsbury station, right the new connection to Abbey Foregate sidings. 1981.

depot and oil tank sidings respectively.

Since closure, the S&M has slowly merged, as is the usual way of such things, into the surrounding countryside though its course is still readily traceable. The most major change so far is probably the new Melverley viaduct, reconstructed in 1962 as a much-needed road bridge; the most unlikely change — and therefore

The Abbey Foregate site today with the oil depot on the left.

the most fitting for this railway — was the temporary use of land at Kinnerley for storing the stock and materials of the Welsh Highland resurrectionists (now based at Porthmadog). Colonel Stephens would have approved.

Will the S&M, in its turn, ever be brought back from the dead? Who knows what the needs and limitations of public and private transport will be 50 years from now? Certainly, in this railway's history, stranger things have happened. And what of the Potts? After the final closure of the S&M the remnants of the Nantmawr branch still lingered on in the hands of BR's Western Region. From 15 January 1951 the former Tanat Valley Light

Railway had been closed to passengers and from 5 December 1960 no goods trains ran westwards beyond Blodwell Junction.

From 1 January 1963 control of what was left of the Nantmawr branch passed to the London Midland Region which closed to goods traffic the Llanfyllin branch from Llanymynech on 2 November 1965 and to passengers on 18 January of the following year. At the same time most of the Ellesmere–Buttington Junction line was closed, with the exception of the link through Oswestry for mineral trains between Gobowen and the eastern end of the Tanat Valley line. Reversing outside Blodwell Junction, these trains still serve the Nantmawr quarries; those same quarries that originally gave rise to the existence of the railway described in this book have survived its closure.

BIBLIOGRAPHY

The S&M has, with just cause, featured in a great many books and periodical articles over the years and the limitations of space prevent a full list. Undoubtedly the most important is:

The Shropshire & Montgomeryshire Railway, Tonks, Eric S. (Industrial Railway Society, 1972)
  Useful back-up works are:
The Colonel Stephens Railways, Morgan, John Scott (David & Charles, Newton Abbot, 1978)
Standard Gauge Light Railways, Kidner, R. W. (Oakwood Press, Lingfield, 1971)
Carriage stock of Minor Standard Gauge Railways, Kidner, R. W. (Oakwood Press, Tarrant Hinton, 1978)

Other background information on the surrounding lines and other Stephens concerns has generally been taken from the various standard works on the railways in question; unfortunately, where the S&M and its predecessors are concerned, much of what has been written often conflicts with other sources; wherever possible this history has been compiled from contemporary accounts and records, official and unofficial.

ACKNOWLEDGEMENTS

We should like to express our gratitude to all those who have so willingly helped us in our research, especially the staff of the Shropshire Libraries and Record Office, and who have kindly permitted the use of many of the illustrations. Special thanks must also go to Philip Shaw of the Colonel Stephens Railway Museum, Tenterden, and to Barry Williams for once again providing the excellent maps.